AGAINST THE ODDS

Malala Yousafzai

Claire Throp

heinemann
raintree

Edited by Linda Staniford and Jennifer Besel
Designed by Philippa Jenkins and Tim Bond
Picture research by Tracy Cummins
Production by Helen McCreath
Illustrated by Oxford Designers and Illustrators
Original illustrations © Capstone Global Library Limited 2015
Originated by Capstone Global Library Limited
Printed and bound in China by Leo Paper Products

19 18 17 16 15
10 9 8 7 6 5 4 3 2 1

Library of Congress Cataloging-in-Publication Data
Throp, Claire.
  Malala Yousafzai / Claire Throp.
    pages cm.—(Against the odds biographies)
  Includes bibliographical references and index.
  ISBN 978-1-4846-2464-7 (hb)—ISBN 978-1-4846-2469-2 (pb)—ISBN 978-1-4846-2479-1 (ebook) 1. Yousafzai, Malala, 1997---Juvenile literature. 2. Girls—Education—Pakistan—Juvenile literature. 3. Girls—Violence against—Pakistan—Juvenile literature. 4. Women social reformers—Pakistan—Biography—Juvenile literature. 5. Taliban—Juvenile literature. 6. Pakistan—Social conditions—Juvenile literature. I. Title.
  LC2330.T49 2016
  371.822095491—dc23   2014050224

Acknowledgments
We would like to thank the following for permission to reproduce photographs: Alamy: epa european pressphoto agency b.v., 37, LatitudeStock, 7; AP Photo: Alastair Grant, 23, Anja Niedringhaus, 20, Queen Elizabeth Hospital, 25; Capstone Press: HL Studios, 6; Corbis: BILAWAL, ARBAB/epa, 31, REUTERS/Gary Cameron, 35, REUTERS/Hoda Emam, 12, REUTERS/Russell Cheyne, 36 Xinhua/ISPR, 21; Getty Images: AAMIR QURESHI/AFP, 22, AFP PHOTO/PATRICK HERTZOG, 38, Anadolu Agency, 40, Christopher Furlong, 5, John Moore, 9, KARIM SAHIB/AFP, 11, Mike Coppola/for Pencils of Promise, 30, Nigel Waldron, 41, Queen Elizabeth Hospital Birmingham, 27, 28, Robert Harding, 13, STAN HONDA/AFP, 14, Veronique de Viguerie, 16, 17, 19; Landov: EPA/Malala Yousafzai PRESS OFFICE, 29; Newscom: Anthony Behar/Sipa USA, 43, EPA/JAMAL NASRALLAH, 39, HRC WENN Photos, 32, Pete Souza/Polaris, 34 Robin Utrecht/Sipa USA, 33; Shutterstock: CS Stock, Design Element; Thinkstock: Andrew Burton, 8, Andrew Burton, Cover.

We would like to thank the following for permission to reproduce quoted text:
pp5, 32, 33 ©Malala Yousafzai from speech given to the UN General Assembly, 12 July 2013; pp11, 27 taken from the book "I Am Malala" by Malala Yousafzai with Christina Lamb (Weidenfeld & Nicholson Ltd, Orion Books, 2013); p29 Reproduced by kind permission of *The Guardian* newspaper, which published "Malala Yousafzai on life in Britain: We have never seen women so free" article, October 7, 2013; p41 Reproduced by kind permission of *The Guardian* newspaper, which published "Nobel peace prize winners say award is a boost for children's rights worldwide" article, October 10, 2013; p43 Reproduced by kind permission of BBC News, which published "Malala: The girl who was shot for going to school" article, October 7, 2013

Contents

Some words are shown in bold, **like this**. You can find out what they mean by looking in the glossary.

Who Is Malala Yousafzai?

Malala Yousafzai is the girl who spoke out about the difficulties girls face getting an education in Pakistan, the country where she was born and where she lived at the time. She put her life in danger for this. Her efforts were so heroic that she is now a Nobel Peace Prize winner.

Taliban rules

Life was difficult for many women in the Swat District, where Malala Yousafzai was born. They had very little freedom, with rules about where they could go and with whom, and even what they should wear. A Muslim **fundamentalist** group called the **Taliban** (see pages 8–9) was powerful in the area and enforced these rules. In January 2009, it said that girls should not be allowed to go to school.

"I speak not for myself, but so those without a voice can be heard. Those who have fought for their rights. Their right to live in peace. Their right to be treated with dignity. Their right to **equality** of opportunity. Their right to be educated."

Malala Yousafzai, speaking at the **United Nations** in New York City, July 12, 2013

THE PASHTUN PEOPLE

Malala Yousafzai and her family are Pashtuns. Pashtuns are a group of people who live in northwest Pakistan and southeast Afghanistan. They speak their own language, called Pashto. More Pashtun people live in Pakistan than Afghanistan. It is thought that Pashtuns moved to Pakistan between the 13th and 16th centuries.

Becoming a target

Malala Yousafzai wasn't afraid to speak out. As a result of the attention that she gained, she became a target for the Taliban. When her family received threats from the Taliban, Malala Yousafzai started traveling to school by bus instead of walking. On October 9, 2012, she was shot in the head by the Taliban on the way home from school. Amazingly, she survived.

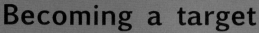

Malala Yousafzai has worked hard to improve children's education around the world.

What Is Pakistan Like?

Pakistan is a country in southern Asia. Pakistan was created after World War II (1939–1945), in 1947, when the country of India was divided to provide Indian Muslims with a country of their own. At first, there were two parts: east and west. In 1971, the east split off and became Bangladesh. An area called Kashmir has caused problems between Pakistan and India ever since. Wars have been fought over which country the area belongs to.

This map shows the main cities and towns in Pakistan.

Landscape

In the north and northwest of Pakistan, one of the world's highest mountain ranges can be found—the Karakoram Range. K2, the world's second-highest mountain, is also in Pakistan. Baltoro Glacier, one of the world's longest glaciers (a very slow-moving river of ice), is also in Pakistan. There are areas of very flat land, such as the Indus plain in the east and the Balochistan plateau in the west.

Swat District, where Malala Yousafzai was born, is in the north of Pakistan, close to the border with Afghanistan. Swat is a long, thin valley, with other smaller valleys branching off it. At one end is Spin Ghar, which means "White Mountain." A mountain called Tor Ghar ("Black Mountain") is at the opposite end of the valley.

Snow and water from the mountains and glaciers flow down to the Swat River.

PAKISTAN FACT FILE

- Country name: Islamic Republic of Pakistan
- Population: 196 million (2014)
- Capital city: Islamabad
- Main languages: Punjabi, Sindhi, English, Pashto, **Urdu**, Balochi
- Main religion: Islam

Religion

Islam is the second-largest religion in the world, and its followers are known as Muslims. Malala Yousafzai and her family are Muslims. Muslims believe in one god, called Allah. They believe Allah sent men—known as prophets—to teach people how to live by his law. The final prophet was Muhammad. The Muslims' holy book is called the Qur'an and is believed to be Allah's words as revealed to Muhammad.

MUSLIMS IN PAKISTAN

Pakistan has the third-largest number of Muslims of any country. Over 96 percent of Pakistanis are Muslim.

Muslims worship at mosques like this one in Lahore, Pakistan.

Armed members of the Taliban can be seen on the streets in some areas of Pakistan.

What is the Taliban?

In 1996, a group called the Taliban came to power in Afghanistan and then moved into northern Pakistan in 2007. The area where Malala Yousafzai lived has suffered a lot of fighting between the Taliban and Pakistani soldiers. In early 2009, the Pakistan government tried to get the Taliban to agree to stop fighting, but the agreement did not last long. Bomb blasts and shootings continue to take place. Thousands of people have been killed.

The Taliban is a Muslim fundamentalist group. This means that followers believe in a very strict reading of the Qur'an and hold extreme views on many issues, such as women's role in life. Their aim is to replace Pakistan's current system of government with an Islamic state, based on Islamic law.

One of the beliefs held by the Taliban is that girls should not go to school. Followers think that educating girls goes against Islamic law. Taliban **militants** destroyed more than 150 schools in 2008 alone.

Politics

The head of Pakistan is the president, while the **prime minister** runs the government. Pakistan has been governed by politicians, while at other times it has been run by the **military**. This has resulted in unstable situations. Since 2007, the government has fought against the Taliban, with little success.

Tradition

In Pakistan, women have long struggled for equality with men. There are many women's rights groups in Pakistan, but they are often targeted by militant groups such as the Taliban. The Pakistan government has been accused of not doing enough to protect the women.

> "I was a girl in a land where rifles are fired in celebration of a son, while daughters are hidden away behind a curtain, their role in life simply to prepare food and give birth to children."
>
> Malala Yousafzai in *I Am Malala*

While Pakistani **traditions** do not usually allow women to mix freely or work, some women have achieved fame in **politics**. Benazir Bhutto was the first woman to lead a Muslim country in modern times.

Benazir Bhutto
(1953–2007)

Bhutto was born in Karachi, Pakistan. She studied in the United States and the United Kingdom. Her father led the Pakistan People's Party (PPP), but he was killed in 1979. Benazir took over the leadership of the PPP and became Pakistan's prime minister in 1988. In 1990, the government was dismissed because it was thought to be **corrupt**. In 1993, Bhutto was again voted into power but defeated three years later. Corruption charges were brought again, and Bhutto and her husband were given prison sentences. To avoid prison, Bhutto went into **exile** in the United Kingdom and Dubai. Bhutto returned to Pakistan in 2007, but died in a bomb blast.

What Was Malala Yousafzai's Early Childhood Like?

Malala Yousafzai was born on July 12, 1997, in Mingora, Swat District, in Pakistan. She was not born in a hospital, but rather at home with the help of a neighbor, because her family did not have enough money to go to a hospital.

Malala's father, Ziauddin Yousafzai, set up a school with a friend. His family lived in a shack with only two rooms, across from the school. Later, they moved into rooms above the school. When she was young, Malala's mother, Tor Pekai, never worked and couldn't read or write. Despite this, Ziauddin discussed everything with her. This is unusual; many men in Pakistan don't ask for the opinions of women.

Who's who

Ziauddin Yousafzai
(born 1969)

Ziauddin Yousafzai was born in Pakistan. He was part of a large Pashtun family, with five sisters and a brother. Part of his passion for education comes from the fact that his sisters were prevented from going to school by his father. He believes girls should be educated and women should be free to do as they wish, rather than be controlled by their fathers or husbands. He ran a school in Pakistan, teaching both girls and boys, and since his family's move to the United Kingdom, he has worked for the Pakistan **consulate** in Birmingham, England.

MALALA OF MAIWAND

Malala is named after Malala of Maiwand, an Afghan heroine. The Afghans, including the man Malala of Maiwand was meant to marry, were fighting the British in 1880. She went to the battlefield to help the wounded, but when she saw the Afghans were losing, she joined the fight. Malala was killed, but she is remembered for her bravery.

The Butkara ruins in Swat Valley are thought to date from the 3rd century BCE. Malala Yousafzai used to play hide and seek there.

Top of her class

Malala would wander around her father's school as soon as she could walk. At the age of three or four, she was put into classes for older children.

Malala was used to being at the top of her class by the age of seven. She was usually in competition with her best friend, Moniba. Then a new girl arrived—Malka-e-Noor—and she was the one who finished first after the year-end exams. Malala was shocked by this—only Moniba had ever beaten her before. She later said, "At home I cried and cried and had to be comforted by my mother."

Malala sits with her mother, father, and brother, Atal.

> "I had the run of the school as my playground… You could say I grew up in a school."
>
> Malala Yousafzai

Brothers

Malala has two brothers: Khushal, who is two years younger than she is, and Atal, who was born five years later. Khushal was named after a warrior poet, Khushal Khan Khattak. Traditionally, a boy is seen as more important than a girl, so Malala's mother was thrilled to have a son. She wanted to buy a new cot for him, but Ziauddin said that the old one was good enough for their daughter, so they did not need to change it.

The Yousafzai children spent most of their time with their mother. Some of Malala's favorite times were when the family had guests come over for dinner and her father would tell stories and read poems afterward.

MALALA'S FAVORITE BOOKS

When she was 10, Malala loved the *Twilight* books. She and her friend Moniba wanted to be vampires!

When Did Malala Yousafzai First Begin to Speak out About Education?

During 2007, the Taliban gained control in Swat Valley. In July, Taliban followers began attacking government buildings, including girls' schools. They believed schools for girls went against Islamic teaching. Malala Yousafzai's school was not bombed, but there was constant fear that it would be.

EDUCATION IN PAKISTAN

In 2009, 68.6 percent of boys in Pakistan (age 15 or older) were able to read and write, but only 40.3 percent of girls.

In Swat District, only a third of girls go to school.

By March 2009, after her blog and public appearances, Malala Yousafzai's life changed as she became well known in Pakistan.

On September 1, 2008, Malala Yousafzai made her first public appearance at Peshawar in front of national press to **protest** against the Taliban attacking girls' schools in July. Her speech was called "How Dare the Taliban Take Away My Basic Right to an Education?" This appearance brought her to the attention of the Taliban.

The Taliban announced that all girls' schools in Swat Valley were to be shut down from January 15, 2009. Ziauddin Yousafzai was asked by an Urdu news company if he knew a student who could write a **blog** about life under Taliban rule. One girl offered to write it, but her parents said no because they feared what the Taliban would do if they discovered the **identity** of the blogger.

Writing a blog

Malala Yousafzai took up the challenge. She wrote under the name Gul Makai, the heroine of a folk tale. It was not safe to reveal her identity. The first entry in her diary appeared online on January 3, 2009. She wrote about her everyday life, especially the way the ban on girls going to school affected her. On January 14, she said she was in a "bad mood" because she may not be allowed to go to school after winter break.

TV and movies

Malala Yousafzai was becoming well known for her opinions on education for girls. She appeared on a popular Pakistani television program in February 2009, one regularly watched by 25 million people. She used it to publicize her views on education and to say that she was not afraid of anyone.

During 2009–2010, two documentaries were made about her by Adam Ellick, a **journalist** from *The New York Times* newspaper. He spent six months with the Yousafzai family. Originally, Ellick had interviewed Ziauddin Yousafzai, hoping to find a family in Swat that was affected by the banning of girls' education. In the end, Ziauddin suggested his own family and daughter. His wife did not take part in the films, however, because of Pakistani tradition. She did not talk to men outside the family.

Forced to leave Swat

Unfortunately, in May 2009, many people living in Swat had to leave as major fighting took place between the Taliban and the Pakistani military. Ziauddin Yousafzai stayed separate from the rest of the family in Peshawar, because he was seen as the main danger to the family. He and three other men from Swat organized protests to try to persuade the government to work harder to stop the fighting.

AN AWARD

In December 2011, Malala Yousafzai won the Pakistan National Youth Peace Prize for supporting girls' education. They renamed it the National Malala Peace Prize in her honor.

The Yousafzais moved four times over the next couple of months. They didn't return to Swat until August. Their schools and city had been badly damaged. Malala Yousafzai's school—Khushal Public School—did not reopen until August, but other schools took longer to open again.

For the National Youth Peace Prize, Malala Yousafzai received 500,000 rupees (about $4,500).

What Happened to Malala Yousafzai in October 2012?

On October 9, 2012, Malala Yousafzai had a Pakistan Studies test. She was worried about it and had stayed up late studying. It went better than expected, and she and Moniba stayed behind at school to talk. They then caught the bus to go home.

When the bus turned off the main road, it seemed quieter than usual. Then a man stepped in front of the bus and asked if it was the Khushal School bus. At the back of the bus, another man asked, "Who is Malala?" Her friends unintentionally gave her away by glancing at her. The man fired three bullets toward them.

Malala Yousafzai shot

The bus driver drove to the hospital in Mingora as fast as he could. Malala Yousafzai and two of her friends had been shot. Kainat Riaz had been grazed by a bullet in her arm, and Shazia Ramazan had been shot in her collarbone and hand. Malala Yousafzai, however, had been shot in the head, the bullet entering above her left eye. It just missed her brain.

Malala Yousafzai was a student at the Khushal School for Girls in Mingora.

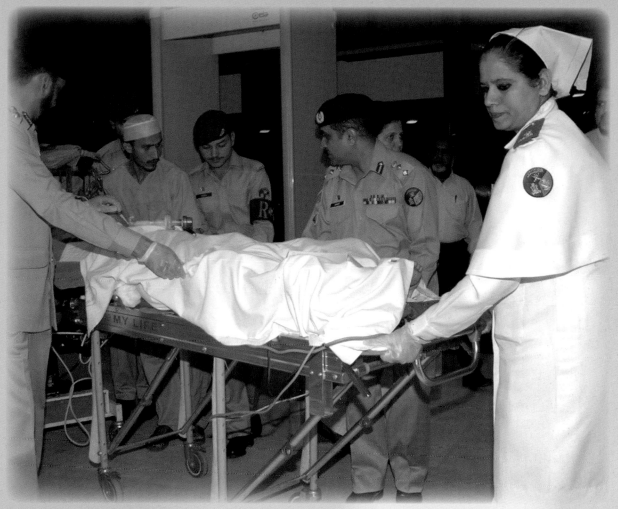

Malala Yousafzai was rushed
to the hospital after being
shot by the Taliban.

A few hours after her treatment in
Mingora, Malala Yousafzai was flown to a
military hospital in Peshawar. Military
surgeon Dr. Junaid Khan monitored her,
and after a few hours noticed that her brain
was beginning to swell. He recommended
surgery to remove the bullet from her body.
Ziauddin Yousafzai was worried at first because he
thought Khan looked too young. It was also very
risky, with the possibility of damage to his daughter's
speech and the right side of her body.

Success

Surgeon Junaid Khan operated on Malala Yousafzai for three hours, removing part of her skull, to give her brain room to expand. The piece of bone was kept in the tissue of her stomach to preserve it, so that it could be replaced at a later date.

The operation was successful. Dr. Fiona Reynolds, one of the doctors who later cared for Malala Yousafzai, said, "I've got no doubt that he saved her life. He's a hero."

People around the world waited to hear about Malala Yousafzai's health. Thousands protested against the actions taken by the Taliban.

Dr. Kayani works at Queen Elizabeth Hospital, where Malala Yousafzai was taken after flying from Pakistan.

After the surgery

Two British doctors—Dr. Fiona Reynolds and Dr. Javid Kayani—were in Pakistan helping to set up a liver transplant program, and they came to see Malala Yousafzai. It was clear that she had been given life-saving surgery, but the hospital was not very modern. Dr. Reynolds was particularly concerned. She recommended that certain changes be made immediately and that the young patient should be moved to a better hospital in Rawalpindi.

Who's who

Fiona Reynolds and Javid Kayani

Dr. Fiona Reynolds was born in Falkirk, Scotland. She has many years of experience working with sick children. She is an **intensive care** consultant in charge of a team of doctors and nurses in the intensive care unit at Birmingham Children's Hospital in Birmingham, England.

Dr. Javid Kayani was born in Pakistan. He was made a consultant in emergency medicine in 1995. He works at Queen Elizabeth Hospital in Birmingham as deputy medical director. He helps to train international medical students.

Moved to the United Kingdom

Doctors in Peshawar refused to move Malala Yousafzai, but the next day it was clear that her health had worsened. The Taliban then admitted that its followers had shot her. Security around the hospital was increased, and doctors discussed how to help her recover properly. Hospitals from all over the world offered care. Eventually, it was decided she would be flown to the United Kingdom for recovery.

On October 15, Malala Yousafzai was taken to Queen Elizabeth Hospital in Birmingham, England. This was where Dr. Kayani worked. Dr. Reynolds worked at the nearby Birmingham Children's Hospital, but she visited Malala Yousafzai nearly every day. Dr. Reynolds was responsible for the young patient during the flight and the first 10 days of her stay in the hospital, because Ziauddin Yousafzai decided to stay with the rest of the family in Pakistan. It was thought to be too dangerous to leave them alone. It then took some time for the Yousafzai family to be able to travel to the United Kingdom.

A HOSPITAL ON A PLANE

Malala Yousafzai was flown to England on a jet belonging to the United Arab Emirates ruling family. The plane had its own hospital on board.

Another operation

On November 11, Malala Yousafzai had another operation. This one was to repair a facial nerve. This nerve helped control things like raising an eyebrow or smiling. It took 8.5 hours. The surgery was successful, but it took about three months before she could start moving the left side of her face again. She had to perform facial exercises every day.

Malala Yousafzai was soon able to sit up and read. She also spent many hours playing Connect 4 with nurses and doctors until her parents arrived in England.

Well-wishers

Malala Yousafzai received hundreds of gifts and letters from people around the world, including two shawls that had belonged to Benazir Bhutto, the first female prime minister of Pakistan and one of Malala Yousafzai's heroines (see page 11). Malala Yousafzai had cards and messages from celebrities, including Beyoncé and Angelina Jolie. She also received 8,000 cards from well-wishers. One was simply addressed to "The girl shot in the head, Birmingham." One writer proposed marriage!

Many people wanted to visit Malala Yousafzai, but few were allowed to. Gordon Brown, who was once British prime minister and was now UN Special **Envoy** for Global Education, visited and brought books for her to read. He told her that he had set up a **petition** under the name "I am Malala," with the aim of getting every child into education by 2015.

"She [Dorothy] had to overcome a lot of obstacles to get where she was going, and I thought if you want to achieve a goal, there will be hurdles in your way but you must continue."

Malala Yousafzai, after reading *The Wonderful Wizard of Oz*, a book given to her by Gordon Brown while she was in the hospital

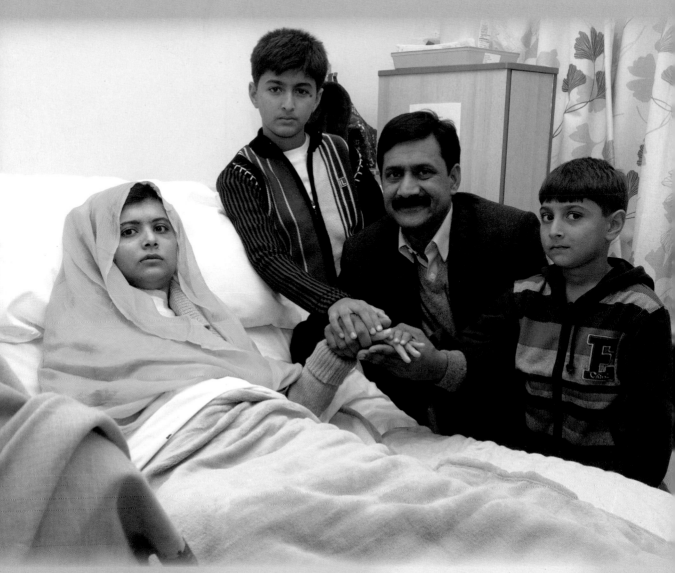

A web page

Queen Elizabeth Hospital set up a special web page to report on Malala Yousafzai's progress, because so many people wanted to know how her recovery was going. It also started a **fund** for her. On the day of doctors' final report about her health, over $15,000 had been raised.

The Yousafzai family arrived in England on October 25.

What Happened After Malala Yousafzai Left the Hospital?

On January 3, 2013, Malala Yousafzai was finally able to leave the hospital. She recorded a video message thanking people for their prayers and telling everyone that she was getting better every day.

More operations

In February, Malala Yousafzai had more operations, including one to replace the bone cut from her skull. Instead of using the original bone, which had been sewn into her stomach tissue to keep it healthy, a titanium metal plate was used. There was a risk of infection if the bone was used. Malala Yousafzai asked to keep the bone after it was decided to use titanium instead. She also had a cochlear implant placed in her ear to improve her damaged hearing.

Malala Yousafzai thanked the nurses who had helped to care for her before she left Queen Elizabeth Hospital.

In March 2013, Malala Yousafzai started at Edgbaston High School for Girls in England.

Life in England

Ziauddin Yousafzai was given a job at the Pakistani consulate in Birmingham for three years, so that he could stay in the country without a **visa**. The family moved into an apartment in the city center and later into a house. Malala Yousafzai went to school at Edgbaston High School in March. Adjusting to life in England was hard for her. She and her family keep up their Pashtun **culture**. She wears a shawl over her head, for example.

"It was difficult to adjust to this new culture and this new society, especially for my mother, because we have never seen that women would be that much free... In our country, if you want to go outside, you must go with a man—if even your five-year-old brother goes with you it's fine, but you must have someone else, a girl cannot go outside all alone."

Malala Yousafzai

How Has Malala Yousafzai's Life Changed?

In November 2012, Malala Yousafzai, Shiza Shahid (see box below), and others set up the Malala Fund to help pay for education for girls in Pakistan and around the world. One focus of the fund is to increase awareness of the difficulties faced by girls in many countries. Another is to link with business to give girls access to education. The first project sent 40 girls to school in Swat Valley, where Malala Yousafzai lived.

Who's who

Shiza Shahid
(born 1989)

Shiza Shahid was born in Islamabad, the capital of Pakistan. She helped other people from a young age, volunteering at a relief camp after an earthquake. At age 18, she moved to the United States to attend Stanford University. While there, she saw a film about Malala Yousafzai trying to bring the world's attention to education for girls. She arranged a summer camp for her and 26 other girls. Shahid took charge of media interest in Malala Yousafzai's life after the shooting.

The Nobel Peace Prize nomination

In March 2013, Malala Yousafzai was **nominated** for the Nobel Peace Prize. She was the youngest-ever person to be nominated. It showed that she was now seen as a respected international figure. She became one of the people whom journalists went to for comments on any stories relating to education or girls' and women's rights.

THE NOBEL PRIZE

Industrialist Alfred Nobel died in December 1896, leaving a will that said his fortune should be given out as prizes for outstanding achievements in physics, chemistry, literature, medicine, and peace. The Nobel Prize was first awarded in 1901.

Malala Yousafzai was one of *Time*'s 100 most **influential** people in April 2013.

Malala Yousafzai spoke at the United Nations Youth Assembly in New York in 2013.

"The wise saying, 'The pen is mightier than the sword.' It is true. The extremists are afraid of books and pens. The power of education frightens them. They are afraid of women. The power of the voice of women frightens them."

Malala Yousafzai

Birthday celebrations at the UN

On July 12, 2013, Malala Yousafzai spoke at the United Nations (UN). The UN is an organization that works to keep peace around the world. It was her first time speaking in public since the shooting. It was also her 16th birthday. She called for free education for every child. The UN announced that July 12 would be known as Malala Day.

Malala Yousafzai wore a shawl that had belonged to Benazir Bhutto. It was the shawl sent by Bhutto's children to her when she was in the hospital. The event was also important because her mother let herself be photographed in public for the first time. Photographing women is not acceptable in much of **conservative**, traditional Pakistani society.

> "Dear brothers and sisters, do remember one thing: Malala Day is not my day. Today is the day of every woman, every boy, and every girl who have raised their voice for their rights."
>
> Malala Yousafzai

International Children's Peace Prize

Malala Yousafzai won the International Children's Peace Prize in 2013, an award she was first nominated for in 2011. It was presented to her on September 6, 2013, in the Netherlands. In her acceptance speech, she pointed out that people in the Netherlands and many other places take going to school for granted—and that's how it should be. She also announced that the prize money of 100,000 euros (about $115,000) would be used to improve girls' education in Pakistan.

Malala Yousafzai received the International Children's Peace Prize in the Netherlands from Yemeni civil rights **activist** Tawakkul Karman.

What else happened in 2013?

While many people around the world waited for news on the Nobel Peace Prize, Malala Yousafzai herself pointed out that winning the prize was not her main aim: "If I don't get it, it's not important because my goal is not to get Nobel Peace Prize, my goal is to get peace and my goal is to see education of every child."

Negative response

In the end, Malala Yousafzai did not win. Her friends in Pakistan had been sure she would win and were disappointed. However, other people in her hometown believed that she didn't deserve the prize. Some people thought that she was a spy for the West, and others suggested she wasn't actually shot at all. Many people did not like her attempts to get girls educated. One worker in a bank said, "She doesn't deserve it [the Nobel Peace Prize] at all... [Her] interviews overseas will not help girls here." Some people thought that if she had won, more girls would have been hurt by the Taliban.

Malala Yousafzai met President Barack Obama and his family at the White House during her trip to the United States in October 2013.

International Day of the Girl Child

Malala Yousafzai visited the United States in October 2013. International Day of the Girl Child was celebrated in Washington, D.C., on October 11. The United Nations created the day to bring attention to girls' rights and the challenges they face globally, especially in education. Malala Yousafzai spoke at the ceremony, telling her story and arguing for girls' education.

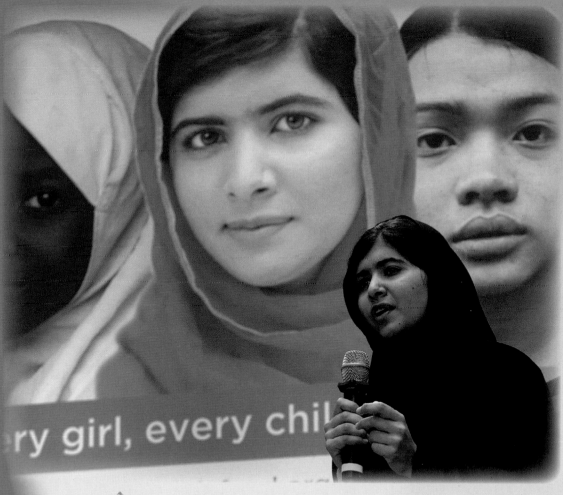

Malala Yousafzai attended the International Day of the Girl Child in Washington, D.C., on October 11, 2013.

Global Citizenship Commission

On October 19, 2013, Malala Yousafzai joined Gordon Brown and many others at the first Global Citizenship Commission at the University of Edinburgh, Scotland. The commission plans to update the Universal Declaration of **Human Rights** of 1948. This sets out the rights that all people should have, such as access to education. Malala Yousafzai gave a speech and then talked with Brown in front of an audience of over 1,000. She revealed that fighting with her brothers was a common event at home!

Malala Yousafzai is seen here with Gordon Brown and Professor Timothy O'Shea at the first Global Citizenship Commission on October 19, 2013. She had been given an honorary degree, awarded for her support for girls' education.

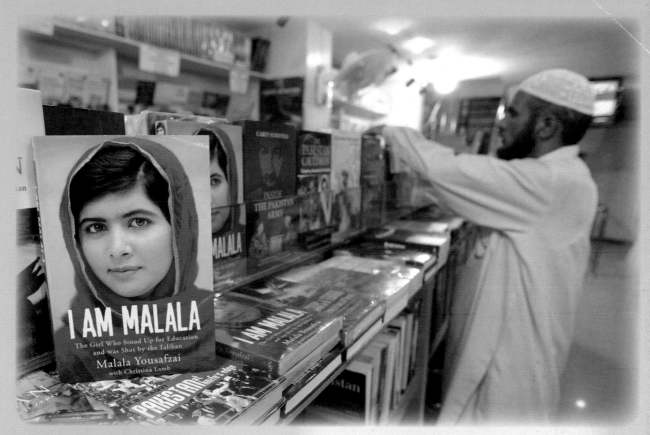

I Am Malala

With help from American journalist Christina Lamb, Malala Yousafzai wrote a book called *I Am Malala*. The book looks at her early life and examines in detail the events of October 2012.

I Am Malala went on sale in Pakistan's capital, Islamabad, in October 2013.

Some private schools in Pakistan refused to have Malala Yousafzai's book in their libraries because they said its negative views of Pakistan would damage students' minds. The Taliban also threatened to attack any bookstores that stocked the book in the Yousafzais' home **province** of Khyber Pakhtunkhwa (KP). A book launch at Peshawar University was canceled because of pressure from local government officials. It is thought that the Taliban forced the university to cancel the event.

Is Malala Yousafzai Still Making News?

There were more awards to come for Malala Yousafzai. In November 2013, she received the Sakharov Prize for Freedom of Thought, Europe's top human rights honor. It was presented to her at a ceremony in France. The award is worth 50,000 euros (about $58,000) and is presented every year in memory of Russian scientist Andrei Sakharov, who won the Nobel Peace Prize in 1975.

Re-educating boys

Malala Yousafzai hasn't always been able to accept awards herself because she was in school. Her father has accepted awards on her behalf. He was also asked to speak at other events, such as the Being a Man festival in London, England, in January 2014. He suggested that re-educating boys to change their views on women was one way to help improve women's lives.

Malala Yousafzai received the Sakharov Prize at the European Parliament in November 2013.

Visiting the Zaatari refugee camp

On February 18, 2014, Malala Yousafzai and Shiza Shahid traveled to the Syria–Jordan border to stay at the Zaatari refugee camp for a week. This was a Malala Fund project to raise money for schools at the camp. Thousands of people who were forced from their homes because of war live there. The fund plans to hire teachers and repair schools—one school for girls and one for boys.

There are only three schools at the camp for about 50,000 children. Some children also have to work rather than go to school because they need to earn money for their family. Families are struggling because aid money raised by people around the world is not getting through. Malala Yousafzai and her father urged world leaders to visit the camp and see what was going on.

Malala Yousafzai spoke while visiting the Zaatari camp in February 2014.

Nigeria

In April 2014, a militant Islamist group called Boko Haram **kidnapped** over 200 Nigerian girls. The group wanted to overthrow the Nigerian government and used bombs and kidnappings to try to achieve that aim. It said it planned to sell the girls. Malala Yousafzai got involved with the attempt to free the girls. She said that the girls were "my sisters" and that people should "not remain silent" about the kidnappings. She suggested that Boko Haram did not understand Islam. The faith encourages all people to be educated and to gain knowledge.

In July 2014, Malala Yousafzai visited Nigeria and met with some of the parents of the missing girls. She also tried to persuade the Nigerian president, Goodluck Jonathan, to meet with the families of the kidnapped girls. Eventually, on July 22, the Nigerian government paid for a plane to take the parents and some of the girls who had escaped to meet the president in Abuja, Nigeria's capital city.

Malala Yousafzai met with families of the kidnapped Nigerian girls to show her support.

The Nobel Prize committee described Malala Yousafzai and Kailash Satyarthi as "champions of peace." The awards were given on December 10, 2014.

Nobel Peace Prize winner

The Nobel Peace Prize of 2014 was awarded jointly to Malala Yousafzai and Kailash Satyarthi, a man who fights for children's rights in India. The two winners agreed to work together to try to protect and educate children everywhere. They also hoped that the award would bring India and Pakistan closer together. Malala Yousafzai is the youngest-ever person to win the prize.

"Through my story I want to tell children to speak for themselves, not to wait for someone else. I stand up with all the children and this award is especially for them. It will give them courage."

Malala Yousafzai

Malala Yousafzai's New Life

From a young age, Malala Yousafzai has fought to bring attention to the issue of girls' education. She was targeted by the Taliban when her blog, television appearances, and awards made her famous. Surviving being shot by the Taliban in October 2012 made her an **inspiration** to even more people. Her speeches and actions have encouraged other well-known people to join in her fight. She has also inspired young girls to stand up for their rights.

Returning to Pakistan

Malala Yousafzai's life has been turned upside down in recent years. She moved to a new and very different country from the one she was raised in. She has said that she would like to return to Pakistan as soon as it is safe to do so.

In 2014, she won the Nobel Peace Prize, which she claimed was for "all the children whose voices are not being heard around the world."

In her book, *I Am Malala*, she says that she does not want to be remembered for being shot by the Taliban. She wants to be remembered for standing up for the rights of girls everywhere. If the Taliban thought they could stop Malala Yousafzai by shooting her, they were wrong. She is now stronger and more powerful than before.

"I think they [the Taliban] may be regretting that they shot Malala," she says. "Now she is heard in every corner of the world."

Malala Yousafzai

Timeline

1997

Malala Yousafzai is born in Mingora, Swat Valley, Pakistan, on July 12

2007

The Taliban gains control in Swat Valley

2008

Malala Yousafzai makes her first speech at a protest against the Taliban in Peshawar, Pakistan

2009

Malala Yousafzai begins a blog for an Urdu news web site, writing about the closing of schools and the right of girls to be educated

2011

Malala Yousafzai wins the Pakistan National Youth Peace Prize

2012

Malala Yousafzai is shot by the Taliban on her way to school on October 9

2013 **MARCH**

Malala Yousafzai becomes the youngest-ever person to be nominated for the Nobel Peace Prize

Malala Yousafzai goes back to school on March 19 for the first time after the shooting. She attends Edgbaston High School for Girls in Birmingham, England.

JULY

Malala Yousafzai celebrates her 16th birthday by speaking at the United Nations in New York City on July 12

SEPTEMBER

Malala Yousafzai wins the International Children's Peace Prize

2014 **FEBRUARY**

Malala Yousafzai travels to the Syria–Jordan border to visit the Zaatari refugee camp for the Malala Fund

JULY

Malala Yousafzai visits Nigeria and meets President Goodluck Jonathan to discuss the Nigerian girls kidnapped by Boko Haram. She also meets with some of the girls' families.

OCTOBER

Malala Yousafzai is the joint winner of the Nobel Peace Prize

Glossary

activist person who works hard to bring an issue or subject to people's attention. This might be through demonstrations, for example.

blog web site on which a person regularly writes news and ideas

conservative having very traditional ideas and beliefs

consulate place where a consul works. A consul is a person who lives in a foreign city and protects the interests of people from his or her own country who live in that city.

corrupt dishonest; often refers to actions taken by people in government or business

culture ideas, customs, and beliefs of a particular group of people

envoy representative of government

equality when everyone has access to the same things, such as freedom or education

exile when a person is unable to live in his or her own country

fund money to be spent on a particular project

fundamentalist person who believes in a very strict version of a religion

human rights things that many societies believe everyone should have— for example, freedom, shelter, food, and education

identity who somebody is

influential having an effect on someone or a group of people

inspiration something or someone that creates a positive feeling in people, encouraging them to do something

intensive care medical treatment for a person who is seriously ill or hurt. It involves the person being constantly watched over by doctors and nurses.

journalist person who writes about the news or who makes films about the news

kidnap take someone by force and ask for something, usually money, before the person will be released

militant person who uses violence to support something he or she believes in

military armed forces, such as the army

nominate put forward a person's name to win an award

petition appeal on behalf of a particular cause, often signed by many people

politics how a country or area is ruled. It usually involves different political parties, or groups of people who have similar ideas and beliefs.

prime minister head of government of a country

protest take action to show disapproval of something

province area of a country with its own local government

surgery treatment of injuries or diseases through operations carried out by surgeons

Taliban extreme Muslim group that wants to set up an Islamic state in Afghanistan and Pakistan

tradition passing on customs or beliefs to the next generation in a family or community

United Nations international organization set up to try to keep peace around the world

Urdu official language of Pakistan

visa document required for people from many foreign countries to live in other countries

Find Out More

Books

Aretha, David. *Malala Yousafzai and the Girls of Pakistan* (Out in Front). Greensboro, N.C.: Morgan Reynolds, 2014.

Doeden, Matt. *Malala Yousafzai: Shot by the Taliban, Still Fighting for Equal Education* (Gateway Biography). Minneapolis: Lerner, 2015.

Rowell, Rebecca. *Malala Yousafzai: Education Activist* (Essential Lives). Minneapolis: ABDO, 2014.

Yousafzai, Malala, with Patricia McCormick. *I Am Malala: The Girl Who Stood up for Education and Was Shot by the Taliban.* New York: Little, Brown, 2014.

Web sites

www.freethechildren.com
This is the web site for one of the charities that Malala Yousafzai supports.

www.malala.org
This is the web site for the Malala Fund.

poy.time.com/2012/12/19/interactive-timeline-malala-yousafzai
This web site has a timeline of Malala Yousafzai's life up to the end of 2012.

Further research

- Try to find out more about the history of Pakistan, particularly the area where Malala Yousafzai was born.

- Learn as much as you can about Islam. What are the Five Pillars?

- What does the Malala Fund do? Research other groups that aim to help empower girls around the world.

- See if you can find out more about the different awards that Malala Yousafzai has won.

Index